Jack and Jill Go Up The Home Ownership Hill

The Home Buyer Checklist You've Been Looking For

Scott Culberson

DEDICATED TO

My wife Kim, our children Gavin and Gillian. My Mom, Dad, sister, in-laws and countless buyers that inspired me to put my home buying ideas into print, so I can help even more people to...
LIVE LIFE TO THE FULLEST!!!

Jack and Jill just moved out of the condo down the way and bought a traditional brick four bedroom, two and a half baths on a hill not far from the subdivision splash park. It may sound like a nursery rhyme…come on think about it for a minute…Jack might not break his crown again if he and Jill owned a home on the hill instead of renting in the valley. Let's take a step back in time a bit and see how Jack and Jill started their REAL Journey….

UP THE HOME OWNERSHIP HILL

It was a day not unlike any other; the sun had come up; Jack and Jill had worked an eight-hour work day and had just settled down at the dinner table for dinner. Let's listen in….

"Jill, that Plum Pudding Pie smells delicious, I can't wait to stick my thumb in it," said Jack with a wink. "There will be plenty of time for pie after dinner. Did you mail the last payment on your doctor bill today," asked Jill? "No, I paid it online this morning before I left for work and it has already posted as PAID IN FULL," Jack said with a smug look on his face. After a rather lengthy pause Jill blurts out: "I want to buy a home on the hill." Startled from his eating Jack sputters, "Where did that idea come from?" With a rosy glow all around her Jill responds, "Jack, if we owned a home on the hill we might not have you getting hurt every couple of months and we could start our family." Jack knew Jill was right and that night they talked and laughed about how happy they would be to own their own home on the hill. The next morning Jack

and Jill ate breakfast with renewed happiness and gusto as they shared in their dream of their home on the hill. Now you need to understand that Jack and Jill were not naive school children, they were smart and they both had good jobs. What they didn't have, was an idea of how to even start their new climb UP the hill. They were quite handy with a computer, so they started to search how to buy a home and they were overjoyed when they ran across...

"The Home Buyer Checklist You've Been Looking for"

And of course, that is exactly what they had been looking for. So, join Jack and Jill as they start their REAL Journey.... UP THE HOME OWNERSHIP HILL.

☐ 1 GET PREQUALIFIED

Deciding that you want to buy a home is not really the first step in home ownership and your path to personal wealth. Before you even start looking at homes, you need to get a prequalification letter(a letter stating how much a lender will lend you based on their guidelines).

Your real estate sales agent can help in choosing a lender to start the prequalification process. Going through the steps to get prequalified will help you decide if this is the right time for you to buy a home. The interest rates may be right and homes may be available, but your financial future may not be ready.... yet. Here's another way to look at it:

You've decided that you want to go on vacation. You have packed the car, got the snacks, boarded the animals, got the mail and newspapers put on hold. Your destination: Disney World in Orlando, Florida. You have your vision, but you haven't looked at all the small goals that have to be met: 1) Are you driving straight through? 2) If you're going to stop along the way, where? 3) Did you book a hotel along the way? 4) Are you going to sleep in the car? 5) Did you book a hotel in or around Disney World? 6) Can your car handle the trip? 7) Can you afford the expenses to go to Disney World?

8) Do you have enough gas? Taking off looking for a home without getting prequalified is just like jumping in the car and heading for Disney World without checking the gas and looking under the hood. Once you check out your car you might find that it won't make the trip, so you change your destination to Sea World in San Antonio, Texas and make it a day trip.

Getting prequalified will make your home buying experience go smoother. The lender will be asking specific questions regarding debt, income, credit history, etc. Gathering the information they will need may take you some time to find. Having your taxes and banking records at your fingertips will help in the process. A lender can advise you on what price range you can afford. Most sellers will not even consider an offer unless they have proof of financing or funds available (bank statement for cash buyers). By taking this step, you will be ready to search homes in **your** price range and have the ability to make an offer when you find that perfect house you want to call home.

Jack and Jill both felt a little bit like their friend Patience Muffet. See, Patience was really afraid of spiders and if she thought one was even coming close to sitting down beside her…she would get scared and run away. That's how Jack and Jill felt…. scared…were they financially ready????????? They weren't ready to find a lender just yet, so they decided to keep reading.

*So, Jack and Jill decided to read all of **"The Home Buyer Checklist You've Been Looking For"** before they started to check off each item one by one...it just made sense to them. They were getting more serious about their pursuit for their own home on the hill and here is what they read:*

☐ 2 *CHOOSE A PROFESSIONAL*

Choosing a **real estate sales agent** is not your full-time job, but it should be the **full-time** job of your real estate sales agent...to be **A REAL ESTATE SALES AGENT**. Real estate professionals have many titles: broker, broker associate, real estate sales agent, real estate salesperson and more. We are going to use the term real estate sales agent for our checklist.

You want someone that is licensed to sell real estate in the state you want to live in. If you have made the commitment to buy or sell real estate, you should have a real estate sales agent that is committed to forming a strong business relationship with you. Here are some for choosing a real estate salesperson:

1) Personal Referrals–Ask your closest friends who sold them their home. Now think about this for a minute. They bought that home five years ago; that's a long time. Your friend will have to think about it and get back with you. They might have forgotten their real estate sales agent because they haven't heard from them in five years. Hmmmmmm, you are going to want a professional that is dedicated to serving your needs–before, during and after the sale. Personal referrals are the best, because you have a friend you trust telling you that this is someone who they trust.

Key questions to follow-up with your friend: Would you buy your next home with this real estate sales agent? Would you sell this home with the real estate sales agent? Trust is the key. Would you want to use the hairstylist of a friend whose hair looks like a rat's nest? If you don't like what their stylist has done with their hair you're probably not going to want that stylist touching your hair.

2) Advertising–Think about the last time you bought something advertised on TV or in a magazine. What were they selling? Did you buy it because it filled a need, or did you buy it for some other reason? Just because a real estate sales agent has a billboard, park bench, TV commercial, shopping cart or Home Owners Association newsletter ad, does not mean their work ethic fits with your personality or needs.

3) Websites, Blogs and Facebook–This is separate from advertising because if done correctly they serve a REAL function. Websites, Blogs and Facebook serve three main functions: information, call to action, and communication. As you are researching for your real estate sales agent: are they providing information, communication opportunities and a call to action? These are all important and useful in your search for a home.

4) Communication–It is EXTREMELY important that your real estate sales agent communicate with you in a way that YOU WANT to be communicated (e-mail, text, phone calls to the cell phone, phone calls to the work phone, phone calls to the home phone, Facebook messages, Twitter tweets, etc.) Who is number one in this situation????? **YOU ARE**, and don't you forget it. Make it a point to find out what communication methods are available for you. If you love to receive text messages, you need to make sure that your real estate sales agent is on the same page. Your real estate sales agent also needs to understand how handy you are with a computer and if you have access to a scanner or fax machine.

5) Home Search–Your real estate sales agent needs to be part of your home search, but not the beginning, middle, and end. Here's what I mean. **YOU** must be an active participant in your home search. To get the home of your dreams you need to be part of the game. So, suit up and get in the game. Your real estate sales agent is a major player, notice that I didn't say coach. You're the player coach. Your real estate sales agent is the player agent, the pinch hitter, the announcer, the cheerleader, the medic and the relief pitcher. They are what you need them to be at that moment in time and sometimes they will be everything at once.

6) Availability–Your real estate sales agent should be available to you on your schedule. You are the client, you are important, and you should be given priority. This is the one way that a full-time dedicated real estate sales agent is different from the part-time real estate sales agent. A part-time real estate sales agent has another job for eight hours a day, when do they have time for you?

7) Eating Real Estate Every Meal–Another way a full-time dedicated real estate sales agent is different from the part-time real estate sales agent is that they are always working on real estate. Their focus is directed at being the best real estate sales agent they can be. They have one vision of success and that is to help you achieve YOUR real estate goals. This can be seen through the weekly improvement meetings that they attend. The professional company they keep. The ongoing education that a full-time real estate sales agent takes is typically more than the State requires. Even the amount and type of information that they provide to potential clients on a regular basis is at a higher level.

These are my seven tips for you based on clients, friends and family. You have a tough choice before you. Somewhere along the way you will need a real estate sales agent. Take the time to learn who you're working with. Ask questions, conduct job interviews. A real estate sales agent that does not want to be interviewed…hmmmmmm…you make the call. It's your dream, who is going to be a part of your team to make it a reality?

"Hickory, dickory, Jill I think we should start looking for a real estate sales agent, right now to help us with our real estate goal" Jack said in a flourish of excitement. "Jack, I agree, but I think we should continue to read all the check points. So far, we need a lender and a real estate sales agent," Jill was cut off by Jack who said, "Yea, it's like we're gonna need all the king's horses and all the king's men."

Jack and Jill are entrenched in the home buying process and every day they are noticing new "For Sale" signs in yards, mortgage company's television ads, and other real estate related happenings. They are in the zone, it wasn't that there were more homes on the market or that the mortgage companies had bought more television time.... Jack and Jill were now paying attention. So, they were excited to read about:

☐ 3 *LEARN WHAT COSTS ARE INVOLVED IN BUYING A HOME*

It's important to understand the closing costs for buying a home, early in the home buying process. You can get that information from your lender or your real estate sales agent. They both will use different tools to illustrate your closing costs and should be pretty close to what ends up on your closing statement (the final documents your sign before you get your keys).

Your lender can provide you with an **INITIAL FEES WORKSHEET** when you work with them on your prequalification letter. After your offer on a home has been accepted by the seller it's time for your real estate sales agent to send a copy of that contract to your lender. Once the lender has the copy of your contract you can formally apply for a mortgage. The government (Real Estate Settlement Procedures Act) requires that the lender provide you with a GOOD FAITH ESTIMATE within three days. The good faith estimate is just what it says….it is their estimate on what it would cost for you to buy a specific home using their lending services. By understanding the title company fees, attorney fees, homeowner association fees and home owners insurance it puts your home buying in a real light of what is paid now to own a home **AND** what will be paid on a recurring basis (home owners association fees, home insurance, etc.)

Your real estate sales agent can also provide you with an Estimated Cost Worksheet that can give you a good starting point. It will give you basically the same information as the lenders initial fees worksheet and is just an unofficial estimate. Home owner association fees and yearly taxes are posted on most Multiple Listing Services information pages, so you may have access to a lot more information than you originally thought. Not all real estate sales agents provide an estimated cost worksheet, and that's ok, your lender is the money person. Your real estate sales agent is the negotiation-home information finding out person and more.

*"Well, Jill did we learn anything from this point on our checklist?" asked a puzzled Jack. "Jack is your head bothering you again? Come on now you need to focus," scolded Jill. "Of course, we learned something. We learned that there are fees involved in buying a home and that we should learn about them by talking with our lender and our real estate sales agent," said Jill calmly. "Yea, I got that too, I guess it will make more sense once we have an **initial fees worksheet** in our hands," smiled Jack.*

*"Come on Jill, can't we just mark off some of these
checkpoints?" asked Jack "Can't we just move on? After all
we KNOW how to search for a home," Jack said in
frustration. "We, as in you, may **THINK** we, you, know
how to search for a home, but I don't see us living in one," Jill
quickly responded. "Jack, it's time you play the part of the
wise old owl and listen, do not speak while I read this check
point out loud."*

☐ 4 *SEARCH & SEARCH & SEARCH SOME MORE*

Homes that are FOR SALE are marketed in
many, many, many different ways. The homes you
find on the internet or in magazines may have already
been sold. The ads for a real estate magazine are
typically gathered months before it hits the shelf at
your local grocery store. You would think the
internet would be up to date because... "if it's on the
internet it must be right." The problem with that is a
lot of the websites that post homes for sale don't
move the homes from Active (available to be bought)

to NOT AVAILABLE (sold or under contract). This can make for a very frustrating home search. The best way to combat this is to contact a real estate sales agent. They have access to the most current information that is not available to the public, which includes those fancy, national real estate websites. Yep, even THAT website does not have the most current information.

Another way homes are marketed is through an OPEN HOUSE. You've seen the signs and you may have even seen the reality real estate shows on television. It's a good way to view a home, but you should not depend on it as your only way to search for a home. Not all open houses are posted on the internet or listed in the local paper, some are just a sign in the yard and that's it. You could waste a lot of gas looking for an open house to view. Again, your best bet is to contact a real estate sales agent and they will be able to provide you with the most current information.

When you meet with that potential real estate sales agent ask if they can set up a home search that meets your needs. When they say "of course" take the time to discuss the things that you have to have in your new home...location, school, size, price (as determined by your visit with a lender), bedrooms, etc. Some real estate sales agents even have a mobile search website for your smart phone. But don't just rely on that search! Search and search and search some more. You can always drive the neighborhood before you call your real estate sales agent for the most updated information. Do the neighbors take pride in their homes? Did you hear a train near-by?

Is that a plane flying overhead; looks to be flying really low? Search, search and search some more. You heard from a co-worker who had a friend that told them that a home in such-and-such neighborhood was for sale and it would be great for you. Give your real estate sales agent that subdivision name and let them provide you with a list of the homes for sale in that subdivision. Lastly, it's ok to change your search criteria, that's why it's ok for you to continue to search, while your real estate sales agent created search is specific to your needs when it was set up. You may decide that you "can't live without" a study or that you "really, really" want a hard-counter surface for the kitchen. Use all your tools available and keep your ears and eyes open...your next home may be right around the corner.

"Can I speak now," Jack asked timidly? "Yes, Jack, I was only trying to make a point," smiled Jill. "You know I have been seeing a lot of FOR SALE signs lately Jill. I didn't realize that it was because we are in the process," Jack stated. "I've noticed the same thing: signs, television ads, even real estate sales agents names on cars," Jill responded. "I wonder how we will find our home," asked Jack? "We will find our home by looking together my dear, and looking and looking and looking," Jill whispered. And they fell asleep with dreams of home searching dancing in their heads.

We return to our heroes Jack and Jill, with Jack returning from his monthly visit to the doctor. "Jill, I'm back, Jill," shouted Jack as he entered their tiny condominium. "Yes Jack, I know you're home, I could hear you when you walked up, through these paper-thin walls," said Jill crossly. "SOOO, get on with it, how was your appointment with Doctor Foster," enquired Jill? "He told me that, yes, indeed, I have a brain and it appears to be mended. ANNNNNND, no more monthly visits," Jack smiled. "Perfect, Jack, it's time for us to dive into our next check point," said Jill eagerly. And this is what they read:

☐ 5 *KEEP AN OPEN MIND*

When you are searching for your next home you **MUST** keep an **OPEN MIND**. Unfortunately, your next home will not come alive and tell you, "I'm the perfect home for you," while trumpets play, and confetti falls from the sky. You will pick your next home by taking the time to research and visit the homes. It is kind of like an interview process...you will interview many before you find the best fit for your needs.

Home buying has also been called home buying through elimination. What do you NOT like about this home? Do you absolutely HATE the front elevation (how the front of the home looks)? Will a couple of cans of paint or some different landscaping change your opinion of the front elevation? If NO is your answer don't take another step, this is not the home for you...strike it from your list and move on. Homes come on the market daily so be open minded to all possibilities.

Home searching overload has hit more than one home buyer and it could hit you, but here are some tips to help you keep an open mind. Don't visit too many homes in one day. Everyone processes information differently, so take notes. The worst thing you could do is create a SUPER HOME in your mind based on bits and pieces of homes you have seen that day. Five homes a day is the magic number.

Also, keep in mind that the home market is NOT standing still while you search for a home. If you view a home today, it could have had five showings yesterday and two written offers already. Because the home market is always moving; when you give your real estate sales agent your list of homes to view give him more than five. One of the homes could already be under contract, while one home is sick with the flu, and another could be hosting a birthday party.

Here's another tip: the photos you see on the multiple listing service and videos the listing agent has made: are to peak your interest to set an appointment, but they also can be used to eliminate a home. No photos or limited photos, something is up...don't waste your time. It's hard to let go of that mystery home that says that it has the right number of bedrooms, square footage, location and price, BUT let it eliminate itself because it doesn't have any or enough photos to deserve your attention. Here's another way to think of it....Up to this point **you** have done everything to prepare yourself to make an offer. You have a pre-qualification letter, you have a real estate sales agent, you have the desire to be a home buyer....Now the homes have to have the equal desire to be sold. So if you see anything that may be deceptive in the marketing of a home, strike it from the list.

Everything happens for a reason, again BE OPEN MINDED, you are looking to eliminate homes. If it is to be it is up to you. **The one house you cannot find enough to strike it from your list, that is the one that YOU will call HOME.**

Jack and Jill now had a clearer picture of how to search for their home on the hill. "Jill, I don't know about you, but I've had an open mind once or twice," Jack said with a wink. "Yes," Jill interrupted, "I remember bandaging that mind more than once with vinegar and brown paper." "Well, I like this new type of open mind much better," Jack said as he leaned in to give Jill a kiss. Jill returned his kiss with a blush.

To say our heroes Jack and Jill were excited about finding their own home on the hill was an understatement. They had the home buying bug...BIG TIME. "Jill, I see that you have our next check point printed and ready to read," Smiled Jack, as he headed to the kitchen table. "Yes, Jack, I have it printed, and the dinner is in the oven staying warm. Let's go ahead and read it, before we eat," sang Jill eagerly. Jack replied, "Sure Jill," and so Jack began reading aloud....

☐ 6 *A HOME THAT SUITS YOUR NEEDS?*

When you are searching for a home you need to look into your crystal ball and see what you will need for a home in the future. Now since the crystal ball store went out of business a couple of hundred years ago it might be a good idea to review your goals for the next five, ten, and fifteen years. The goals you need to review are personal, work and relationship. In other words, your goals for you, your goals for your job, and your goals as a couple. All three should meld together at some point. If one of your work goals is to be CEO of your company in five years and

19

that company just happens to have their headquarters in another state...well, that is why you need to go through this exercise. Respect for your spouse's personal dreams and needs for fulfillment are just as important as yours. That's what makes two people into one. Now if you are single; but have a main squeeze it might be time to have serious talks about where the two of you see things going. No pressure, no worries, just reality. Buying a home is a commitment for the next five to fifteen years. That's why you need to review those long-term goals. Things happen, and situations change. You may want to move closer to family if a loved-on falls ill. Or you may get an unexpected promotion with the division your company just bought that moves you to another state. Life happens, so be as prepared as you can.

What will you need IN your home to satisfy your needs in the future? That definitely varies from buyer to buyer, but the basics remain the same...you need a home that has strong bones, has room to grow, and you are proud to come home to. The home structure we will talk about in a later check point. You will want room to grow in your home, but be careful not to overdo it. A couple with no pets and no children might not want to buy a five-bedroom home...yet. Or maybe they do if they know that they have family that will be visiting for long periods of time or they don't have a study or game room. In this case the extra bedrooms become the study and the game room, which leaves you three rooms for beds. Human nature is to fill available space with stuff. Be aware of this trap and work hard to keep it in check, A four-bedroom home is a perfect size for a couple that doesn't have kids or a dog, yet. One bedroom is the master, two bedrooms are for guests and one is a study/hobby room. That doesn't mean that each guest room needs a full bedroom suit. Sometimes a blow-up mattress works just fine. After all, if your guests don't leave you won't have a chance to miss them.

So as Jack finished the last sentence he walked to the kitchen. On the way he slammed his knee on the counter. "Yowie, that hurt," Jack yelled in pain. "I know one thing is for sure, we need a bigger kitchen, especially since your cooking is getting tastier and tastier, Jill. Before long I won't be able to fit in this kitchen," Jack said with a grin. Jill met his smile and they set the table together, working hard not to bump Jack's sore knee again. That night they started on their short and long-term goals.

*Jill was dripping wet when she entered their tiny
condominium. A shredded umbrella in one hand and a bag of
Chinese takeout in the other. As she closed the door her heel
gave way and down she went. Fortunately, it was a tiny
condominium, and Jack was able to catch Jill before her fall
did her any harm. Jill began to cry as she tried to talk "Jack,"
sniff, "I," sob, "just," sniffle, "want to be able to park outside
our home," Jill cried on, not in pain, but from the wet and the
sadness of the broken heel on her shoe and the further
realization that their parking situation would not get better
until they had their own home on the hill. Jack handed her a
towel, a warm cup of tea and said, "You relax, I got the food
warming in the oven, dry off, drink your tea and I'll read."*

☐ 7 *WHERE DO YOU WANT TO LIVE?*

I don't know, where do you want to live? I
don't know, where do you, think we should live? It's
a discussion that people have been having for years.
When you're looking for a home, unless you have
some type of restriction that you have placed on
where you want to live, the world is your oyster.
Surely you don't want a two-hour commute, one way,

uphill, in the snow. Or maybe you have to have that type of commute because you want to live by a lake or have your children go to a certain school. Location **IS** the biggest question in real estate and that's why everyone will tell you it's the first, second and third most important thing, so location is important, but it's not just the State or the city, or the subdivision, or the school district, it can also be the street. Do you want your home on a corner, a cul-de-sac, on acreage, next to the park, or far away from the park? When you are searching you should look at the satellite view of the homes that peak your interest. The satellite might show vacant land, a creek, a river, railroad tracks, a salvage yard or strip center that you didn't see when you drove to the property. Keep in mind that land that is vacant now may not be vacant forever. Farmer McDonald may decide to sell that vacant land and you don't have any control over who he might sell to. Can you get to work from your new home? Is there more than one route? Is there a toll road within a couple of miles that would make your commute a little bit easier?

By the time Jack finished reading Jill had cheered up, dried off and the food was ready to eat. Jack spoke, "Jill I am making it part of our home search to find us a home that has covered access from the car to the kitchen. I never want you to have to worry about getting soaked or slipping or..." Jill cut him off saying, "Thank you sweetie." And with that she kissed him on the scar of the side of his head and handed him a plate of Chinese food. They ate in silence as the storm rolled through.

Jack had just pulled away from their condominium. When Jill pulled out the next check point. Jack frowned. "What? It's a thirty-minute drive and it's only a couple of lines long." Jill said with a lilt in her voice. "OK," said Jack. "But don't quiz me when you're done." So, Jill began to read....

☐ 8 *NEGOTIATE WITH KNOWLEDGE*

This is probably the check point that most readers will skip. I am sorry to report that there is no magic bullet or crystal ball. The best asset you have for negotiations is your real estate sales agent. Take the time to review the contract template your real estate sales agent wants to use BEFORE you start looking for a home. Understand all the negotiation points and timelines. Knowledge is your friend and the more you understand the negotiation points in the contract the better you can respond in the heat of the battle. That's why the two Super Bowl teams practice before the Super Bowl...it's so they understand what their opponent is going to do in a situation, so they can be at the RIGHT PLACE. AT THE RIGHT TIME and then...TOUCHDOWN!!!

Let's back up a little and talk about when your negotiation starts. It doesn't start when you like the home, or after you have put in an offer. YOUR negotiation starts when you first start to read the Multiple Listing Service information with your real estate sales agent. There are subtle clues in the general listing and sometimes more in the agent remarks (available only to real estate sales agents) that could help you formulate your game plan from the very beginning. This doesn't seem like much of a negotiation; the seller is basically telling us what type of financing they will accept and that they are keeping the ceiling fan in the bedroom and so on. Understanding the hard lines the seller has drawn will help you to decide if you can live with those terms or if you want to buy a home from a seller that might be a hardliner throughout the process.

Did you have trouble making an appointment to see the property? Did they move the showing time? Did they shorten the showing time? Did they give a reason for making changes to the appointment? Were they reasonable reasons? That's subjective, I know, but if a child is sick or they have family in town...that's ok.

It's nice to know the reason why the property is being sold, but it is not your right to know. Sellers guard their reason for selling very heavily and it is within their right to do so. The worst thing you could do is visit a home in search of the upper hand instead of seeing if this could work as your next home. Negotiations are meant to be in the best interest of both parties.

What the seller sees as value, you may not. The buyers set what is valuable by buying homes they like. Those sellers that don't move with the market, i.e. change their selling price or fix problems with the home, will be left behind. Days On Market(also known as DOM) is often seen as an indicator of urgency to sell. Your real estate sales agent can help you with these when he gathers the competitive market analysis for that subdivision. It may be that homes in that neighborhood sell slower or it may be that the seller is holding the line. Let your real estate sales agent go over the competitive market analysis with you in person and in detail. This is what they do for a living and it is not as cut and dried as you may think. You really need a detailed competitive market analysis to understand what direction you should take your negotiation.

"I guess I was really hoping there was a magic bullet to the whole negotiating thing," Jack said with a sigh. "Knowledge is Power, my dear," Jill said with a wink.

Jack and Jill were enjoying warmer temperatures with a long walk in the valley. They walked hand in hand, and Jill had a mischievous grin on her face as they approached a park bench. Jack, knowing his bride, took a seat and waited. Jill's smile grew as she began to read...

☐ 9 *CONSIDER A HOME PROTECTION PLAN*

Various things may go wrong with your home. Home protection plans do NOT cover all repairs so it's important to understand what is covered and what is not. They are usually purchased for a one-year term. The home protection plan(also known as a residential service contract, or a home warranty) can give a home buyer the peace of mind that if something were to happen to their home that they can call their home protection provider and have it fixed at a reduced cost. Costs are involved and that is part of figuring out which plan is best for you. If you have an in-ground pool, you'll probably want to make sure that it is covered in your home protection plan and to what extent.

Talk with your real estate sales agent about a

home protection plan. You might be able to structure your negotiations so that the seller pays for your home protection plan. Or maybe the seller is already offering a home protection plan as a value to you, the home buyer. Minimal investment, yet a huge piece of mind. Do your homework; check out the different home protection plans available in your area. You want a home protection plan with a local service team.

"Wow, Jill that sounds like a micro-insurance plan that places a protective bubble over our home," Jack said. "I've read about these before Jack, they can save us big money if we have the right coverage and our air conditioner goes out," smiled Jane. "Short, but informative, that's the kinda check point I like," winked Jack and they continued their walk.

Jack had accomplished his mission. The mission was to surprise Jill at work with lunch and a little light reading. Jill blushed when she came to the front of her office and saw Jack with a hand full of food and a balloon that said " I Love You Because You're You". With a bubbly smile Jill said, "This is a great surprise sweetie and you're going to read to me. You're the best!" So off they went to have a little picnic lunch and to read....

☐ 10 *GET A HOME INSPECTION(S)*

To have home inspection(s), you need to have a licensed home inspector. You can find one by asking your real estate sales agent, doing an internet search for your area or using the phone book. Do you still even have a phone book? The reason you want a licensed home inspector is that his license holds credibility with regard to the report they prepare for you. They are bound to check a long list of items dealing with how your home functions. This magic list changes slightly from year to year, but typically works in conjunction with the building code for the largest city in the area...that is if the town you are in doesn't have its own building codes. This does not mean that a home built in 1988 has to match the building code of a home that was built this year. This year's building code is the benchmark that a home is graded against. The inspection list grows and changes which is why it is REALLY important to have a licensed home inspector perform your home inspection(s).

The home inspector is required to annually update his education so that he is familiar not only with current code, but reoccurring issues to look for in homes. A basic home inspection is usually completed within the first fifteen days of the contract period, depending on what you negotiated with the seller. The home inspector provides a written report to the buyer and the buyers real estate sales agent (with the buyer's permission). The buyer, after all, is paying for the expertise of the home inspector.

The seller must allow you the ability to perform the home inspection(s) within a timely manner. All utilities must be on in order to have a proper home inspection…that's gas, water, electricity. Who pays for those to be turned on is negotiable. If the seller is still living in the home, it is usually not an issue. If you are buying a foreclosure you will have to have your real estate sales agent, ask the foreclosure bank for permission to turn on the utilities.

You can have many different types of inspections on your new home and not all basic inspectors are qualified to complete these "other" inspections. Here's the short list: mold, swimming pool, structural, septic system, and more. **You should get a home inspection even if this is the 100th home you have**

bought. It gives you a heads up on the things that are not working now and in some cases, it might show the need to have additional inspections like a structural inspection that you would want done by a structural engineer. It is also a good idea to be present during the inspection. Your report will be detailed and will even come with photos of the issues with your home, but it REALLY helps if you can be there for the inspector to show you first hand.

So, the inspection is done, the inspector either prints the report on site or you will receive an email in the next day or two. Not all inspectors complete their reports on site so if you are in a rush you might have to pay a little extra for that luxury. Once you receive their report you should review it with your real estate sales agent so that you can decide your next move…continue buying the home or negotiate some specific repairs. If you ask for repairs, make sure you ask for the repairs to be done by a real repairman and also ask for receipts for those repairs. Your inspection is the proof in the pudding that there is something that needs to be fixed. There is no: "he said, she said." You hired a professional home inspector and his license binds him to his work.

This is a home your buying, it's a BIG deal, you want your repairs to be done right the first time. For an additional fee, most home inspectors, will re-inspect to verify that your repair requests were done to the code that he graded them on. A home inspector is a great resource of knowledge for your home. Bring a note pad, pen and questions, your inspector will be glad to answer them.

"So, the home inspector checks out your home for you, wow that's cool," Jill said. "Well, he comes with a price tag, but it sounds like it's money well spent. I mean if we really want the home, I think we really want a home inspection before we go all in and buy the place," Jack responded as he walked Jill back to work. "You made my day Jack," Jill said as she kissed him on the scar on his head. Jill went back to work full of food and feeling loved and Jack was curious about the next check point.

Jack jumped out of bed that Saturday to find Jill standing by the window of their tiny condominium, coffee in one hand the next checkpoint in the other. "Oh, Jack, I know that all the check points are important, but this one really hits home," snickered Jill. Jack laughed at her pun as she started to read....

☐ 11 *Research Your Home Insurance Options*

You must have insurance for your home especially if you are purchasing it with a loan. Your lender wants their investment to be protected and let's be honest, so do you. You are looking for a homeowner's policy and if you do not pick one your lender will, and it will be much more expensive than any policy you would find on your own. Do not wait until the title company asks for your insurance company, start shopping now. Lots of insurance companies will bundle car, life and home and give you a discount. If you have never thought about changing your car insurance, now is the time to check out what is out there. You'll see lots of television ads and billboards, what do you really want from your insurance company? Do you want twenty-four-hour claim service, the ability to pay on line, the discount rate mentioned above? Meet with your insurance agent and talk with them about this new step in your life, you may find that you don't have as much coverage as you thought on your car or on yourself. Yes, yes, yes, more homework and if you take the time now, if something bad happens in the future, you'll be covered.

"WOW, that does hit home," Jack said, and they laughed at the pun again. "If we didn't have insurance for all those times you got hurt coming down that hill, I don't know where we would be," Jill replied. "I guess it's time to review ALL of our insurance since we are on the home buying trail," Jack said. And as they pulled their insurance files they were eager to read the next check point.

Morning, noon and night Jack and Jill were reading their checklist points and gathering the information they needed to be informed home buyers. "Jill," Jack said pausing then continuing, "I think it's a good thing we are reading these checkpoints because I have no clue what this one is all about." And without allowing Jill to respond Jack began to read....

☐ 12 *The Appraisal*

The appraisal is the value that the lending bank has applied to the real estate that is being purchased. An appraisal will be ordered by the lending bank on the real estate that you have an executed contract on. The lender typically orders the appraisal AFTER you have done all your tire kicking (inspections, and repair negotiations).

Here's the bottom line on an appraisal...the subject real estate HAS to appraise for equal to or higher than the contract sales price. If it does not you are back to the drawing board with the seller. This is one of the reasons you discuss the competitive market analysis at length with your real estate sales agent. The competitive market analysis DOES NOT take the place of an appraisal, but it can give you some insight into what the appraiser might come up with. Your real estate sales agent and the appraiser, in all likelihood, will be using the same comparable homes and both should have a similar approach as to what to do with those comparable homes. The appraisal from YOUR bank rules the day, even if the seller had an independent appraisal done on their home. Should the home not appraise(make value) the seller or buyer could dispute the results. In today's market most appraisals stand because of all the checking and double checking the appraisers do now.

"Jack, I don't think I would have known that's what this checkpoint was about," said Jill. "Good information, and it makes since. The bank wouldn't want to lend money on real estate that doesn't at least equal the amount of the home they are lending on," Jack said as he shook his head. "Kinda makes your head hurt doesn't it, Jack? It's pretty deep stuff," Jill responded. And so, our two heroes were getting closer to the last check point. Their anticipation was growing.

Jack slammed the door when he came home, and their wedding picture hit the floor with a smash of glass. "Whoa MR, you march right back outside and try that entrance again," Jill said crossly. Jack and Jill had decided, when they were dating, that they would never bring home the frustration they had gained at work or where ever. Sure, they would talk about it, but no taking it out on the door or each other. "Sorry dear," Jack replied, "My day well...its' better now that I have come in for the second time." And that's one of the small things they did together that they both truly loved and respected. So, Jack closed the door gently, picked up the next checkpoint from the kitchen table and read.......

☐ 13 *Right Before You Get the Keys*

Every contract has a closing date on it. Most contracts say something like "On or before this date." This date is the date you have been waiting for. It's time to look at what happens before you get the keys.

About a week before the special day (this timeline can vary) your title company will receive the closing instructions from your lender. The title company takes those instructions and prepares the initial CLOSING DISCLOSURE (aka closing statement). The CD as it's commonly called contains all of the charges for the buyer and the seller and its format is uniform. Your lender and your real estate sales agent will be familiar with the format and how to explain the various charges. The preliminary CD goes to your lender and the seller. They are both checking to make sure that all the numbers are correct. Your lender gave the instructions to the letter. Once the two parties agree the FINAL CD is generated. This does not mean that the CD is perfect...you should always review your final CD; you may find that the changes you thought were being made have been missed. Compare your CD to the Good Faith Estimate that your lender provided. The final CD tells you the amount you need to bring to the closing. That will be in a cashier's check (certified funds) and in most cases, it is payable to the title company since they distribute all the funds. NOTE...ASK WHO TO MAKE YOUR CHECK OUT TO and get the spelling right. If the cashier's check is wrong in name or dollar amount you will not be able to get your keys. Some title companies will allow you to have your closing check wired to their account instead of having to bring a cashier's check. Wiring funds is tricky, make sure you get written instructions from the title company at least five days prior so you can execute those directions carefully.

To get your keys from here there are six final steps:

1)   Verify that you walked through the home prior to closing and that it is as you expected it to be

2)   Receive any receipts from agreed upon repairs

3)   You present your portion of the money in the form of a cashier's check (certified funds)

4)   Your lender has wired their money to the title company and the title company has confirmed receipt (aka the file has funded)

5)   The seller(s) signs their portion of the closing documents and presents a photo id

6)   You, the buyer(s), sign your portion of the closing documents and present your photo id(s)

It is important to note that not all closings will fund the same day, which means that you may not be able to walk away with the keys that day. You will still own the real estate, but think about it; the title company must get the money from your bank, payoff the sellers mortgage and pay the real estate sales agents and themselves. Nothing is truly final until everyone gets paid.

Your closing will probably start on time, and it will take some time to get through the paperwork. Your closer will present you the papers to sign, one by one and can explain what you are signing and answer your questions. It's your closing so take the time to read what you sign, don't feel rushed. Your closing could take a couple of hours so it's better to take the rest of the day off from work. Title company's handle the six steps above in different order and some title companies have fresh cookies and some have gourmet coffee. But you're not buying cookies, you're buying real estate. Once all the steps have been completed....

CONGRATULATIONS
YOU'RE A HOME OWNER!!!

"I love me some fresh cookies," Jack said. "Cookies or no cookies it sounds like we might need to practice signing our names, so we don't get a cramp," Jill said with a smile. "Jill, do you realize that this is the second to the last checkpoint," Jack asked? "I guess class is almost over. We are fixing to graduate from home buyer novice to home buyer," Jill said with a grin. And that night they made their own fresh cookies, peanut butter, chocolate chip and a chocolate peanut butter that didn't turn out so well. They were finding that the checkpoints were helping them to become less fearful of the home buying process. They knew they needed help, lender, home inspector, and their own real estate sales agent. They were truly ready for the final check point.

"Jill, I feel like the picture of the little home sitting on top of the question mark we saw once. Except, I feel more like Humpty Dumpty right after he fell. I feel confused and disoriented," Jack said as he placed his left hand with a pointing finger to his puzzled mouth. Just like that picture. *"Silly Jack, Humpty wasn't confused,"* Jill scolded. *"He knew someone would come to help him and if he had some help on the front side he probably wouldn't have fallen off the wall in the first place."* They both laughed and began to read......

☐ 14 *Ask Questions & Understand the Answers*

This checkpoint is more about follow up and understanding the information you receive than it is about a special laundry list of questions. Some answers are easy: Who owns the home now? How old is the home? How many bedrooms? But what about the vacant land behind the home? What about the creek around the corner? What about the schools? How long will my commute be? What about that drain in the front of the home? What about that green box in the back yard? Can we build a pool? Can we raise a pig? OK, so there are a couple of questions for you to chew on. Your real estate sales agent can help you find the answers to almost any question that you can come up with on a piece of real estate. Make it a point to address your concerns before you put an offer on a home.

One last bit of advice from, yours truly, a broker associate, real estate sales agent that has successfully sold real estate for over ten years. When you're looking for your answers don't leave it up to neighborhood gossip. Your future neighbors may feel threatened by you, so they might not give you the real scoop. Everything on the internet is not true; so, any answers you find, you'll want to discuss with your real estate sales agent. Your real estate sales agent may have already heard the rumors in the subdivision and know where to get the REAL answers.

If you have a question about your future home....Ask it early and get an answer. This will be YOUR HOME so take the time for due diligence. It is your job to ask the questions and your job to understand what those answers mean....

DON'T WAIT TIL THE LAST MINUTE TO ASK A QUESTION. Again, ask your question(s) early and understand the answers before you move on to the next item on your list.

Well, you already know how the story ends.

Jack and Jill followed the checklist and found their happily ever after.

Jack will no longer tumble down the hill.

He and Jill are King and Queen of the Hill.

That's the end so here's:

THE HOME BUYER CHECKLIST YOU'VE BEEN LOOKING FOR

☐ 1) **Get Prequalified**

☐ 2) **Choose a Professional**

☐ 3) **Learn What Costs Are Involved**

☐ 4) **Search and Search Some More**

☐ 5) **Keep an Open Mind**

☐ 6) **A Home That Suits Your Needs?**

☐ 7) **Where Do YOU Want to Live?**

☐ 8) **Negotiate with Knowledge**

☐ 9) **Consider a Home Protection Plan**

☐ 10) **Get a Home Inspection(s)**

☐ 11) **Research Your Home Insurance Options**

☐ 12) **The Appraisal**

☐ 13) **Right Before You Get the Keys**

☐ 14) **Ask Questions & Understand the Answers**

I hope that you enjoyed the book.

If you have any specific real estate questions I would love to personally help you with your real estate needs.
You can email me at: Scott@ScottCulberson.com

Please share this book with your family and a friend or two and maybe YOU can help them to...

Live Life to the Fullest!!!

ABOUT THE AUTHOR

Scott Culberson has been successfully selling real estate for over ten years in and around Houston, Texas. He is an Eagle Scout and still supports scouting that is centered around a scout led troop. His favorite authors are Og Mandino, Stephen King, Jon Gordon and the list goes on and on. When he is not spending time with his family or selling real estate you can find him teaching a real estate continuing education class, working in the community, recording a video blog or reading a book.
He is always looking for ways to help people to...
Live Life to the Fullest!!!